SO-CTX-041

"YOU CAN SAY THAT AGAIN"

Cultivating New Life
in Time-worn Christian Sayings

By Richard A. Lundy

ARGUS COMMUNICATIONS A Division of DLM, Inc.
Niles, Illinois 60648 U.S.A.

For allowing us to print an excerpt from *Death Be Not Proud*
by John Gunther, Copyright © 1949 by John Gunther, we
gratefully acknowledge Harper & Row Publishers, Inc.
Reprinted by permission.

Cover design by Don Walkoe
Photographs by Jaime Montemayor

FIRST EDITION
© 1980 Argus Communications
A Division of DLM, Inc.

Printed in the United States of America.

Argus Communications
A Division of **DLM,** Inc.
7440 Natchez Avenue
Niles, Illinois 60648 U.S.A.

International Standard Book Number: 0-89505-051-X
Library of Congress Number: 80-67556

0 9 8 7 6 5 4 3 2 1

Contents

Preface

Words of Faith
Recycled

Words, if we are not careful with them,
wear out and lose their power. If we speak
them too often or use them too flippantly,
they cease to communicate. That's especially
true with words we use to speak our faith—
they wear thin and wear out. These
meditations are an attempt to recycle some
worn-thin words of faith. They are written
in the belief that words that have worn out
should not be thrown away, but need to be
reclaimed by having life poured back into
them again.

There was a time in my life when as a
preacher I didn't think the effort was worth
it. The old phrases had been used so often by

so many people who seemed to mean so many different things that the old words seemed to me to be more barrier to than vehicle for communication. So I threw them out and tried to find new words to give voice to my faith. I've discovered that the old words are too precious to throw out. I want them back again, even the ones that have become cliches.

These meditations are my attempt to recycle and reclaim some wonderful old phrases of the faith. They are offered in the hope that the words may speak anew to convey some of the wonder and mystery of the Christian experience, which is far too rich for any language to capture fully.

RICHARD LUNDY

1

"God Bless You"

We continue to use worn-out words
without much thought, and eventually we
begin to use them in a variety of confusing
ways. That's surely true of the phrase "God
bless you." A sneeze in public is likely to
produce a "God bless you" in reply.
Do something helpful, and you may get back a
"God bless you for what you've done."
The words appear on plaques in houses,
"God bless this house" or "God bless this
mess." Some folks "say the blessing" before
they eat. And we sing "God Bless America"
at patriotic gatherings. The words are spoken
as a benediction—"God bless you and keep
you." Since the phrase is used in a variety of
different settings and seems to imply a variety

of different meanings, let's think for a moment about what we are doing when we ask God's blessing.

We are praying, of course, and hoping that God's favor will come to those we name—this house, this country, these people. The words are a prayer asking God to favor those we care about. It's a most legitimate hope, but it raises all kinds of interesting questions about God's relationship to us. Does God favor some and not others? Do God's blessings come as rewards for work done, lives lived, promises kept? Most of us would say that we hope so; we hope that God rewards faithfulness.

We share that hope with the people of the Bible. They too were forever hoping that their faithfulness would be rewarded with God's blessing. The fact that the blessings seemed so few and far between was one of the things that bothered biblical people most. They kept asking why it was that the "wrong" folks seemed to be reaping all the rewards while the faithful were usually in such dire straits. To ask it in their language, "Why do the wicked prosper while the righteous suffer?"

The Old Testament prophets answered the question in two ways. They suggested that

the "righteous" were not really all that righteous after all; that is, they didn't really deserve God's blessing. And they suggested that someday everything would work out right, that both they and we would get our just deserts.

Jesus, who had a way of turning things around, said that the "rain falls on the just and the unjust alike." (In a parched land rain is always a blessing.) By using the rain as a symbol of God's dealing with us, Jesus demonstrated that blessings are given to everyone, regardless. This meant that they are not rewards after all, but gifts. So maybe being "blessed" doesn't have much to do with being rewarded, but everything to do with being gifted. As the old hymn says, we are to "count our blessings," to number the gifts. Jesus invites us to acknowledge that every last one of us is "rained upon," or blessed. Blessings, then, are not God's way of saying "Thank you," but gifts which come as a prelude.

The Bible makes it clear that as prelude, blessings are to be used. They are God's way of equipping folks for service, of preparing people to be a blessing to others. So, then, to ask God to bless the food and fellowship around a table is to pray that the strength gathered there will be used for service. To ask God to bless a house is to pray that it will be a home in which no one will remain a stranger. To ask God to bless America is to pray that we will be a country in which justice is in fact just and tempered with compassion. It is to pray that our country will be a blessing to other countries. To ask God to bless our loved ones is to pray that they will be equipped and used.

The biblical record makes it very clear that it's when we take the gifts and try to hoard them, to keep them all to ourselves, that we lose them. It's when we pretend that blessings are rewards we deserve and so fail to share them that they are likely to slip through our fingers. Blessings are equipment to be used or they will be lost.

The biblical record also makes it clear that anything which equips or prepares us for service can be a blessing. Anything that invites us to be open to others, to grow in our ability to share the pain of another, anything which serves to sensitize us to a human need is a blessing.

Sometimes people report that an event in their lives was a "blessing in disguise," meaning they have discovered that the

11

event equipped them for more creative and compassionate living. To be sure, it is often difficult to find the blessing hidden in all of the disguise. But almost everything can serve to equip us for more creative and courageous living. That's not to suggest that tragedy is not tragic, but that it can be transformed and used.

So maybe being blessed doesn't have much to do with being rewarded, but everything to do with being gifted. And maybe the gifts are not simply things we want, like prosperity and health and happiness, but are all the events, both good and bad, through which God seeks to prepare and equip us to be agents and instruments of his compassionate love. If so, then God bless you.

2

"Jesus Saves"

The attempt to recycle time-worn words sometimes requires us to come at them from an entirely new direction. That's true, I believe, of the phrase "Jesus saves." It appears on so many bumper stickers, has been scribbled on so many walls, is proclaimed from so many neon signs that it's become a cliche. So, too, with the formulas used to complete the meaning—"from sin," "from death," "from the fate of the lost." All that is true enough, but it is a truth that may have become mute. We can begin to recycle the phrase by looking at an account of Peter and Jesus walking on water found in Matthew 14:22–33.

According to Matthew, Jesus had attracted a huge crowd. The folks had become hungry and Jesus had fed them, all five thousand, with plenty of food left over. After that he asked his disciples to get into a boat and to leave for the other side of the lake while he dismissed the crowd. When the crowd had left, Jesus went up on a hillside to pray. The disciples were out on the lake having a terrible time in a storm. Night came and the disciples were rowing for all they were worth when they saw something out on the water. Thinking it was a ghost, they were terrified.

The figure on the water spoke. "Take heart, it is I; have no fear." Peter responded, "Lord, if it is you, bid me come to you on the water." The figure said, "Come." Peter got out of the boat and walked on the water until he noticed the wind and the waves again and began to sink. He called out, "Lord, save me." Reaching out, Jesus caught hold of Peter, saying, "O man of little faith, why did you doubt?" They both got into the boat and the wind ceased.

What are we to hear in that account? According to the usual interpretation, we are to hear that when the waves of life begin to overwhelm us, we may call out to the One who is present in the midst of the storm to save us. "Jesus saves." Let's look more closely.

As we noted, the story in Matthew follows an account of the feeding of five thousand people (Matthew 14:13–21). In that story it is obvious that Jesus had expected his disciples to be able to feed the crowd. When they claimed to be unable to do so, Jesus himself fed the crowd, seeming to say in effect, "Look, this the way you do it." Then he sent them off in the boat by themselves. The implication is clear: they are going to be on their own. But they let the storm get the best of them. Yet, when Jesus called Peter, he got out of the boat and walked on the water. What a contrast! Only the day before, Peter and the other disciples had been unable to feed the crowd. Now Peter is walking on water!

When Peter began to sink and Jesus reached out and caught hold of him, Jesus said, "O man of little faith, why did you doubt?" What was it that Peter had doubted? That the figure was Jesus? That Jesus would be able to rescue him? I think not. Jesus seems to accuse Peter of doubting his own ability to walk on the water, to stay afloat. Jesus saved Peter from

drowning only because Peter had become frightened and lost confidence in his own ability.

The same incident is reported in Mark's gospel (Mark 6:45–52). Mark ends his report by saying that the disciples were "utterly astounded, for they did not understand about the loaves," that is, about the feeding of the five thousand the day before. What hadn't they understood? They had not understood that Jesus had expected them to be able to feed the crowd, just as he had expected them to be able to still the storm and had expected Peter to be able to stay afloat.

Now then, let's return to our theme— "Jesus saves." The incident of Jesus and Peter on the water surely affirms that Jesus is present in the midst of life's storms to rescue or save us when we are frightened and about to go under. But the incident also affirms that Jesus saves us by having great confidence in our ability . . . to feed the hungry and to still the storms of life.

When the disciples told Jesus about the five thousand hungry people, he said, "You feed them," assuming that they had the power to do so. When Peter said, "Let me come to you on the water," Jesus said,

"Come," assuming that Peter could. In the account, Jesus "saved" Peter not only when he rescued him from drowning, but also when he called upon him to overcome his fear and to get out of the boat, onto the water. Perhaps we need to be saved as much from our fears and from the limitations they place on us as we need to be rescued from our failures.

At any rate, I'm sure that those of us who are sure about things that can't be done need to be saved from our certainty. Jesus saves us by assuming that we can do far more than we believe we can do. He saves us by calling us to feed the hungry and to still the storms of life that threaten to swamp us all.

3

"Praise the Lord"

I have the feeling that sometimes people
use the phrase "Praise the Lord" as a way of
brushing off the expressions of appreciation
that come their way. "Don't thank me; thank
God." In some ultimate sense everything does
come from God. I become annoyed, however,
with some forms of Christian talk which
seem to imply that God gets all the credit for
everything good that happens. The rest of us
are left with nothing but blame for all the
happenings that aren't so good.

It is hard enough for me to love myself and
to love others without language which invites
me to strip us of all good qualities by
suggesting that God gets all the credit or
"praise." I suppose that people who are

quick to say "Praise the Lord" don't intend to suggest that God gets all the credit and we all the blame, but it surely sounds that way. Especially when you consider that many of us have trouble accepting praise.

In being taught that it is wrong to think too highly of ourselves, many of us have learned to feel uncomfortable when appreciative words are spoken to us. We brush them off. "Oh, it was nothing at all. Anyone would have . . ." Lots of us have trouble accepting praise. And yet most of us want it very much. We need and want to be appreciated, listened to, and taken seriously. Maybe that's what the Lord wants, too.

What does it mean to praise the Lord? I suspect it may involve much more than saying the right words at the right time, that it may have something to do with the quality of our responses to God. For example, I'm not sure how to praise someone and ignore him or her at the same time, nor how it would be possible to give a person lots of praise and then refuse to follow his or her lead. All such praise would surely be called "empty." It seems possible, doesn't it, that praise has much more to do with the attention we pay and how we do it than it does with what we say or sing.

The Old Testament prophets were always trying to convince people that God doesn't really want a lot of fancy fanfare and isn't too interested in "testimonial dinners."

> I hate, I despise your feasts,
> > and I take no delight in your
> > > solemn assemblies.

* * *

> Take away from me the noise of
> > your songs;
> to the melodies of your harps I will
> > not listen.
> But let justice roll down like waters,
> > and righteousness like an
> > > ever-flowing stream . . . says the Lord
> > > (Amos 5:21-24).

They kept saying that God is much more interested in faithful living and in peaceful relationships between and among people. Of course, the prophets and some of the people knew that it is far easier to hold a praise service than to commit ourselves to living and doing God's will. It is always easier to heap praises on someone, God included, than to be about the hard tasks ourselves.

I am all for praising the Lord daily if it means acknowledging what the Lord has done—called us and equipped us for service.

I favor daily praise—if it means paying close attention to the One whom we honor, if it means listening to the Lord to learn what we are called to be and do, if it means taking the Lord's advice through such things as taking up our own crosses and following him.

As one who preaches regularly, I become a bit frustrated with folks who are full of praise for my "wonderful sermons" but seem to ignore their implications. If I may be so bold, it seems to me that the Lord must be a little tired of hearing our words of praise and seeing so little action. Of course, such action is far more difficult than telling the Lord how wonderful he is.

Many of the people whom Jesus met were eager to praise him, to tell him how wonderful he was. Yet he kept on trying to empower them, to convince them, that they were far more able than they thought. He kept on calling them to follow him, to join him in being about his Father's business. And he keeps on calling us to praise God, not only with our lips, but with our lives. Praise the Lord!

4

"Born Again"

There is lots of talk these days about "born-again Christians," people who can point to a particular moment or time when they had a religious experience which has led them to divide their lives into periods before and after that event. "Once I wasn't, now I am." Those in the Christian church who are unable to point to a particular time or to a special experience often find it difficult to understand or to appreciate what their fellow Christians are talking about and are sometimes put off by the label "born-again Christian." So let's look behind the label to see if we can reclaim the meaning and promise behind the words.

The phrase comes from a conversation

reported in John's gospel between Jesus and a Pharisee named Nicodemus (John 3:1–15). It's a report of conversation on two levels. Coming to Jesus at night so he wouldn't be seen, Nicodemus acknowledged that Jesus was, as we would say, "a man of God," but seemed reluctant to be involved with him. Jesus responded by telling him that it's impossible to understand unless one is born anew. Nicodemus chose to take Jesus literally and to say, "But that's impossible." Jesus replied by telling him, in effect, that he shouldn't be such a literalist, that he, Jesus, was talking in symbols.

There is no indication in the report of their nighttime encounter that Nicodemus left understanding any more than he had when he arrived. But according to John's gospel, after Jesus had been crucified and Joseph of Arimathea had made arrangements for his burial, Nicodemus showed up again, this time in broad daylight, with oils to be used in preparing Jesus' body for burial. Maybe he did come to understand the symbols after all.

Jesus talked to Nicodemus about "being born of water and of the Spirit." That's a clear reference to baptism. In Jesus' day (and in some churches today), the act of baptism involved being submerged—buried—in water and then being lifted out of the water again. It is a symbol of death and birth. Paul made the symbol explicit when he wrote, "You were buried with him in baptism, in which you were also raised with him through faith . . ." (Colossians 2:12).

Since the action of baptism is symbolic rather than magical, we are invited to ask about its meaning. I suggest that the symbolic action speaks of our need, if we are to live freely and fully, to come to terms with death—our own death, the deaths of those we love, and eventually the death of everything we value.

As nearly as we can tell, we are the only creatures who live with an awareness of death. We are the only ones, therefore, for whom death appears as a threat or, as Paul wrote, "the enemy." The awareness that one day we shall die, be no more, cease to exist, is not only frightening to contemplate, but seems to undercut the conviction that we are significant, that your life and mine count for something that endures.

Death is such a problem, such a threat, that we unconsciously spend our lives trying to hide from its reality and trying to find ways to overcome its finality. It is this need to "beat death at its own game" that accounts

for most of the drivenness of human life.
We all work so terribly hard to make a name
for ourselves, a name that will last.
We support causes, give ourselves to
ventures, join together in groups in the hope
that they, at least, will endure, in the hope
that our influence will survive. We assert
ourselves, hoping to "be somebody." We join
with others in trying to build things—
monuments, businesses, governments, and
nations—that will last. Almost everything
we do individually and collectively can be
interpreted as a heroic shout into death's
void: "Hey, look at me! Look at us! We count
for something! We matter! You can't get us!"

The trouble is that our heroic efforts to
overcome the finality of death, to prove our
eternal worth, to make names for ourselves,
to "beat death," lead not only to marvelous
creations but to terrible destruction. We
human beings are by far the earth's most
creative and destructive creatures. Finally,
we have amassed enough power to destroy
everything we value, perhaps even the earth
itself. And we live now with the awareness
that we may in fact do so. Our seeming
willingness to risk total destruction in the
attempt to protect ourselves from death stems
not from the fact that we are evil or foolish,

but from the fact that we are frightened, frightened by the finality of death and driven to try above all else to survive.

In responding to a frightened Nicodemus, Jesus said, in effect, "You can't really live freely and fully by trying to hide from the reality of death, your own and your loved ones'. You've got to come to terms with it, live through it, and come to embrace a new context for living, to be born again into a reality which transcends death."

The reality to which Jesus pointed with the symbols of water and the Spirit, of death and resurrection, is the affirmation that our personal worth is given to us by God. God declares each of us to be of infinite value. Our significance, therefore, is not destroyed by death. The conviction that God bestows value on us sets us free from the need to prove our value in the face of death, sets us free from being driven by our fear of death to try to defeat it. The conviction that our significance rests in God's hands therefore liberates us to live freely and fully.

That discovery is really like a new birth, a new beginning point for living. For some of us the awareness came in a moment of intense emotional release, like a surrender. For others the awareness of God's affirmation of us comes gradually. However it comes, it comes as a gift. It is not something we can make ourselves believe. That would be but one more heroic effort to "beat death." It is not something we can will ourselves into accepting. The awareness, the discovery, the gift, comes just as life came to us the first time—not of our own doing. The invitation is not to make ourselves believe, but to let it happen.

Listen to Paul, who wrote from within the reality of new life. "None of us lives to himself, and none of us dies to himself. If we live, we live to the Lord, and if we die, we die to the Lord; so then, whether we live or whether we die, we are the Lord's" (Romans 14:7-8). So wrote one who was free to live, to live a free and creative, nondriven life because he knew to whom he belonged in death and in life. It is God's affirmation of us that offers us new life, an affirmation that transcends the threat of death.

To be "born again" is to live in the amazing awareness that our lives are lived in the context of God's eternal love, a context in which death is still very real but not final.

34

The New Testament record does not tell us very much about Nicodemus, except that he came to talk with Jesus one night but didn't seem to understand. And that he was there soon after Jesus had been crucified, and stayed to be of help. Maybe that's when it "happened" for him. At least, it's been that way for lots of folks.

5

"In God We Trust"

We proclaim it on our coins: "In God We Trust." But what does it mean to trust God? A car coming into the intersection from your right skids on the ice and crashes into your front fender. The driver apologizes for crumpling your fender. When you ask him for the name of his insurance agent he smiles and tells you that he's a "believer" and "trusts God." "Sorry, no insurance." A person of faith or an irresponsible fool? What does it mean to trust God?

You attend a lecture on the worldwide population explosion and hear an hour of frightening statistics and projections about overpopulation. During the question period a young man gets up and says, "I don't know why you are so pessimistic. The future is in God's hands. Trust him." The young man's friends applaud. Do you sink down in your chair and hope that nobody knows you're a Christian? What does it mean to trust God?

As a college student you are trying to get to know your new roommate. You discover that she's very suspicious of people, won't let you or anyone else come to know her, keeps to herself except when she's trying to convince you that you need to come to her church and learn to trust God as she does. Do you celebrate her faith or worry about her emotional health? What does it mean to trust God?

You go to another lecture and listen to the speaker tell the audience that if we are going to survive as a nation, we've got to learn to trust the experts and put them in positions of power. The speaker says that's our only hope; trust the experts. Do you applaud him or does he scare you? What does it mean to trust God? Well, these examples are enough to help us discover that the content of the phrase "In God we trust" may be a bit ambiguous.

Historically, to acknowledge that it is in

God that we place our trust was to say something negative, something about what or whom we didn't trust. In the early days of our republic, "In God we trust" meant, by implication, "In the king of England we do not trust." The founders of our nation were unwilling to trust anyone or any group with ultimate power, for they knew that no one and no group was beyond corruption. So they organized a system of government in which power was to be shared and balanced—"In God we trust, not in a king nor in a ruling class nor in an imperial president."

When we are told that we've got to learn to trust the experts, to let them run the show, most of us become a bit uneasy, for we know that even the experts are fallible and corruptible. We would also be uneasy, to say the least, if the military were to take over the government, asking us to trust them to do what is best for us. To affirm that we place our trust in God is to affirm that we do not place our ultimate trust in anything less than God—not in a king nor in politicians nor in scientists nor in the army. "In God we trust," then, is a way of saying whom or what we don't trust, at least not for very long or with very much.

That's part of the point Jeremiah was
making when he wrote,

> Cursed is the man who trusts in
> man. . . .
> He is like a shrub in the desert, . . .
>
> *   *   *
>
> Blessed is the man who trusts in
> the Lord, . . .
> He is like a tree planted by water, . . .
> for it does not cease to bear fruit
> (Jeremiah 17:5–8).

Jeremiah lived in a day when his tiny nation
was saying to itself, "We'll be okay; our
future will be secure; we don't have to worry
as long as we are friends with Egypt. Egypt
is strong enough to protect us. Let's trust the
Egyptians." Jeremiah said, in effect, "If we
place our confidence in Egyptian power,
sooner or later it will get us into trouble."
And he was right; it did, and the nation was
destroyed.

For Jeremiah and the other prophets, to
trust God was to take God's word and will
seriously—the promise and the condition.
"I will be your God and you will be my
people, if you keep my commandments."
That is, "If you will order your lives in ways
that are just and humane, things will go well
with you—not always, but in the long run—

if your commitment is to justice and peace and to the well-being of all people." To say it in our language, those biblical people were committed to the notion that might does not make right, that power alone will not protect. For there is in the world a moral order, God's will, so that one day the oppressed will be free and the oppressors will have their power taken away. It was then, and is now, a gigantic leap of faith, the conviction that trust has more standing than error and will have its day, that love is stronger than hatred and will ultimately triumph, that righteousness is rooted in the way things are and will flower in ways that evil will not.

For Jeremiah the call to trust God was a call to risk living a life committed to God's cause—peace, justice, dignity, and human welfare. The call to trust God has nothing to do with standing by and shirking our responsibilities but has everything to do with committing ourselves to a life in harmony with God's will. The driver who didn't purchase collision insurance because he was trying to "trust God" was irresponsible. God is not in the business of protecting the faithful from auto accidents. Trusting God does not remove us from the responsibility of worrying about the future nor of doing something about it. God is not in the business of taking care of the future that we refuse to care about. Most of us would worry about a roommate who says she trusts God but is suspicious of everyone else.

To trust God is to risk living in the reality that God defines, to risk living in the reality of God's will and love, to live the love that is offered to us and asked of us. To trust God is to risk losing our lives with the assumption that God's will and way make sense because they are rooted in the way things are, and to commit ourselves to the doing of his will and the living of his way, even when this seems to be very costly.

6

"He Is Lord"

It's probably the first claim the early
Christian community made about the One
they remembered and knew to be present in
their fellowship, Jesus of Nazareth: "He is
Lord." The title had a rich heritage; it had
been used in the Old Testament as a name for
God. It was also a title for those with
political authority: "The emperor is lord."
And it was used when describing someone
who owned property or people. Slaves
addressed their owners as "lord."

In New Testament times, the term *lord* was
in common usage. People knew what they
were saying and hearing. It's one of those
words, however, that has dropped out of our
everyday vocabulary. We don't talk of lords

except when we are talking about Jesus. So we need to begin with words we do use.

Even though we don't like to admit it, most of us are followers. Consciously or unconsciously, we choose people to follow, folks who become our authority figures. We listen to them, pay attention to what they say, take their advice, imitate their style. Sometimes we even try to become copies of those we have chosen to follow. Such folks are called *mentors* or *leaders*.

Sometimes, as you know, our trust in our mentors or leaders is betrayed. We discover that we have chosen the wrong person, listened to bad advice, decided to imitate a style that leads us down the wrong road. "I thought he knew what he was talking about, but I was wrong . . ." "I trusted her judgment, and look where it got me."

Choosing to follow someone's advice, to trust someone's leadership, is a risky business. The more of ourselves we commit, the more there is at stake and the greater the risk. When you ask a stranger for directions to the nearest hardware store, placing your trust in him does not involve a great deal of risk. If he gives you a "bum steer," all you've lost is a little time. When you decide to trust the person who tells you that the ladder is secure, the risk is higher. When we set out to follow One who claims to make sense of life, to have *the* clue, the risk is very high indeed.

The Christian faith claims that Jesus of Nazareth is a mentor or leader, an authority figure who can be trusted, who won't betray us. He is One in whom we can risk placing our confidence, a person whose directions we can follow, whose style we can appropriately imitate. He is One to be listened to, who will make sense of us and of life. In fact, the Christian faith claims that Jesus is *the* authority figure above all other authority figures: "He is Lord of lords." Our faith invites us to trust Jesus, to be loyal to him, in the same manner that we are to be faithful to God. Or to say it another way, Jesus is the content of what God wills. We are invited to look to Jesus, to what he said, how he lived, to his priorities and his style, to discover what it is that God wills and what it is that we are to be and do as people trying to be faithful to God. That's why a title that had been used for God came to be used for Jesus.

It's easy to write about such trust, but difficult to live it. For one thing, we cannot slavishly imitate Jesus. He lived in a setting vastly different from our own. The New

Testament account of Jesus does not provide us with ready-made answers to most of the hard everyday decisions we are called upon to make. It is not easy to know what Jesus would have done. Nor is it clear that that's the way we should ask the question about what we are to do. What is clear is that the focus of Jesus' life—God's kingdom—and the style of his life—passionate concern for others, especially the dispossessed—are to be the focus and style of our lives. The Christian faith does not give us a book of rules to obey; it offers us a Lord to know and to follow.

Discovering what it is that the Lord wants us to do is a difficult task. It requires as much information as we can gather about Jesus. After all, it is hard to follow one who is a stranger to us. And it usually requires "checking out" our decisions with others who are also attempting to know and follow him. Most of us have a tendency to fool ourselves into thinking that the Lord wants for us what we want. Psychologists call that projection. We project our own desires onto our leaders and then follow them, telling ourselves that we are being faithful to them when in fact we are simply doing what we want to do. So we need the correction of feedback from others who are also attempting to be faithful to the same Lord.

The really hard part, however, about following this One whom we claim is Lord, comes from the fact that we are all tempted to serve other lords too. Some of us live as if our own happiness or personal welfare were the lord of our lives. That is, we make decisions about what we will do or will not do, risk or not risk, in the light of our commitment to our own happiness. "It would make me unhappy to visit them, so I won't go."

Some of us function as if the family is lord, and therefore comes first. "I always try to do what's best for the wife and kids." Noble, but sometimes the Lord may ask us to make decisions for which our family must pay dearly. Others function as if our country is lord. "Right or wrong, I'll serve." The attempt to be loyal to the Lord Jesus requires us to look beyond our own happiness, to commit ourselves to a community much larger than our families or even our nation.

We are back, then, to the claim "He is Lord of lords." He is Lord of everything else that we are tempted to put first. The only Lord large enough for life.

The suggestion that we refill the term *Lord* with life by beginning with words like *mentor* and *leader* may not capture all the first Christians meant by the claim "He is Lord." We move closer to their meaning when we suggest that he is "Mentor of all mentors," and therefore the One to follow before all others, the One whose priorities and style are the content of what God wills. There·is surely more, but that's enough for starters. After all, Jesus told us that what we call him is not what counts. It's what we do, who we follow, that matters!

> Not everyone who says to me, 'Lord, Lord,' shall enter the kingdom of heaven, but he who does the will of my Father who is in heaven (Matthew 7:21).

7

"God's Will"

The phrase "God's will" is used in a variety of different ways. Sometimes it is spoken in a way which sounds as if God's will is a reality which needs to be accepted, as when people are trying to come to terms with failure. "We'll just have to accept the fact that it wasn't part of God's will." The words are often spoken in an attempt to provide comfort when folks are faced with a tragedy, such as the death of a child. "I hope you can understand and accept God's will." At other times the words are used to describe something we are to discover and do. "I hope you can discover what God wills you to do." Is God's will a reality we must learn to accept or a call we need to discover and follow?

Most of us have a deep need to make sense of things, to know or believe that we live in a meaningful world—a world in which things happen according to plan, a world in which there is a rhyme and a reason behind everything that happens. We want to believe, most of us, that whatever happens fits in, has a place, and is somehow part of God's will.

Furthermore, there is in us a desire to believe that we live in a universe that is not only meaningful but moral, a context in which good is rewarded and evil is punished. That's the assumption behind the question which so often pops into mind when some terrible tragedy strikes us. "Why me? What did I do?"

The same question is also asked when unexpectedly wonderful things happen to us. "Why me?" It's the same assumption: what happens happens as a part of God's moral will—rewards and punishment alike. We want to believe, most of us, that whatever happens somehow fits into God's plan or will, but also that God's will is moral. To say it a little crassly, we hope that faithfulness pays off. Or a bit less crassly, we want to believe that God is partial, that God looks out for the faithful.

According to Matthew, when Jesus was teaching his disciples about the need to love their enemies he said a most surprising thing about God.

> But I say to you, Love your enemies and pray for those who persecute you, so that you may be sons (and we need to add "and daughters") of your Father who is in heaven; for he makes his sun rise on the evil and on the good, and sends rain on the just and on the unjust (Matthew 5:44–45).

Said Jesus, in effect, "God gives the sun and the rain to everyone, regardless. God shows no partiality." Jesus' teaching about God's impartiality raises serious questions about all of our attempts to make sense of things by explaining them with the phrase "God's will." His teaching about God's impartiality undercuts the assumption behind our question "Why me?" And this same teaching raises questions about the wisdom of trying to explain tragedy by learning to accept God's will.

As a pastor I've never buried a baby whose death I was prepared to say God willed. God will help parents cope with a tragedy,

maybe even transcend it, but for me the death of a baby is not part of God's will.

Instead of assuming that God has a hand in everything that happens and that, even though we cannot understand it, everything must fit somehow into God's will, we may believe that like us, God is sometimes helpless. It might help if we believed that things don't always go God's way. When we stop to think about it, they don't go his way very often, it would seem.

Some of the things that happen in life are just plain "god-awful," senseless and absurd. It may be far more helpful to admit that this is so than to try always to put a good interpretation on tragic events by trying to understand them as part of God's mysterious will. God stands with us in the midst of tragedy and shares our sorrow, but much of what happens, God does not will and want. John Gunther's book *Death Be Not Proud*, is a moving tribute to his teenage son, who lost his battle with a brain tumor. At the end of the book Mrs. Gunther writes a few paragraphs about her son's death and God's will.

Since Johnny's death, we have received many letters from many kind friends from all parts of the world, each expressing his condolence in his own way. But through most of them has run a single theme: sympathy with us in facing a mysterious stroke of God's will that seemed inexplicable, unjustifiable and yet, being God's will, must also be part of some great plan beyond our mortal ken, perhaps sparing him or us greater pain or loss.

Actually, in the experience of losing one's child in death, I have found that other factors were involved.

I did not for one thing feel that God had personally singled out either him or us for any special act, either of animosity or generosity. In a way I did not feel that God was personally involved at all. I have all my life had a spontaneous, instinctive belief in the reality of God, in faith, beyond ordinary belief. I have always prayed to God and talked things over with Him, in church and out of church, when perplexed, or very sad, or also very happy. During Johnny's long illness, I prayed continually to God, naturally. God was always there. He sat beside us during the doctor's consultations, as we waited in the long vigils outside the operating room, as we rejoiced in the miracle of a brief recovery, as we agonized when hope ebbed away, and the doctors confessed there was no longer anything they could do. They were helpless, and we were helpless, and in His way, God standing by us in our hour of need, God in His infinite wisdom and mercy and loving kindness, God in all His omnipotence, was helpless too.

Mrs. Gunther's convictions are in harmony with Jesus' teaching about the impartiality of God's love. They are in harmony with the image of God reflected in the cross, an image of a God who knows our suffering and shares our pain. We need to be careful about saying too quickly or too easily that things need to be accepted as part of God's will. Maybe God is as frustrated and as angry and as grief-stricken as we are!

Rather than trying to explain things by using the phrase "God's will," we need to be about the business of trying to discover and do his will. The Bible makes it clear that God has hopes and dreams, a plan and purpose for the creation, and invites us to join him in helping to fulfill them. The Bible makes it clear that God calls us to be instruments and agents of his will, to be about the tasks that love and justice and the making of peace require.

The rough outline of what God wills us to be and do is clear enough, but sometimes the specifics are not very clear at all. In fact, there is plenty of evidence that many people who thought they were doing God's will were wrong, at least about the specifics. For example, in the early days of New England the good church fathers who burned the witches at the stake were sure they were doing God's will. Today we know that those women were bearers of a prophetic faith the good church fathers didn't want to hear. Many of our great-grandparents who moved West and drove the Indians off the land were sure they were helping to fulfill God's will for America. With the wisdom of hindsight most of us are not so sure. The recognition that others have been very wrong about the content of God's will invites us to acknowledge that we may be wrong too. That's especially true when we are likely to benefit in ways that others won't from what we hope is God's will. We need to be careful not to confuse God's will with our own.

The fact that others have been wrong about what God wills and that we may be wrong too does not, however, remove from us the responsibility of trying to discover and to do God's will. It simply puts us in the difficult place of trying as best we can to be faithful to God's magnificent will for all of creation—and for us, too—while remaining open to the possibility that we may be wrong about the specifics. Maybe that's part of what it means to "live by faith!"

When Jesus went to Jerusalem it became clear to him that what he wanted and what God wanted were not quite the same thing. Yet he chose to do what he believed God wanted him to do: "Nevertheless, not my will but yours be done." Which is a way of saying that Jesus lived by faith too. Is God's will a reality we need to learn or a call we are invited to discover and follow? Far more often it is the latter!

8

"God Loves You"

"God loves you"—the most fantastic claim of all—is spoken so often and so easily, mouthed so casually, that for many of us it often has no meaning at all. When you stop to think about it, even for a moment, it's a stupendous claim, almost too good to be true; too magnificent to believe—that God, the Creator of all that is, the Power and Presence behind the universe, loves you. Too magnificent to be believed unless it is experienced, this love.

What's so all-important about the experience of love, about being loved? Answer: We were created that way, to be loved, and we can't really live without love. There is clinical evidence, for example, that

65

infants deprived of the experience of affection, who are reared in settings in which they are neglected or ignored, suffer both mental and physical deterioration. Babies who are not cuddled or talked with are often stunted in their growth, and they sometimes die. We are made for relationships, we need to be loved if we are to live.

All of us therefore spend our lives, spend ourselves, trying to find what love promises: a sense of worth, the awareness that our lives are of some value, that there's a place where we belong, where we count, that somebody knows our names and cares. We spend our lives trying to find what love promises— worth, value, significance. We spend our lives!

We may try to find what love promises by driving ourselves, trying to convince ourselves and other people that we are worthwhile and significant. We drive ourselves in order to make a name for ourselves. "See, I am somebody." We write books, get our names in the papers, build monuments. We struggle to do important things that will be noticed and remembered. We have children. Almost everything we do can become a driven search for what love promises.

Some of us bend over backwards trying to be good enough to be loved. We do more than is expected. We struggle to be virtuous. We try to please almost everybody. We keep all the rules, do what's right and proper, trying very hard to be acceptable. On the other hand, some of us are so desperate for approval that we sell ourselves, will do almost anything, will violate almost everything we value, in the hope of finding loving approval.

Many of us live with the conviction that we've got to be perfect to be loved, or at the very least, that we have to keep on trying hard to be perfect. We push ourselves toward perfection, trying to measure up. Almost everything we do can be a search for what love promises to give us, an attempt to win our worth, to prove our value, to demonstrate our significance, to merit love.

But the tragedy is that almost everything we do to make ourselves worthy of love tends to keep us from accepting the love that is offered us. For example, the conviction that we have to measure up in order to be worthy of love leads us to the conclusion that we aren't good enough to deserve love. Or if we are very good at deceiving ourselves, we may convince ourselves that we do measure up and therefore deserve the love that is offered. But when love is accepted as a reward it loses its impact.

Oftentimes our desire to merit love, to be good enough or lovable enough to deserve love, leads us to deny everything within us that seems negative or unacceptable. For example, if we live with the conviction that it's not all right to be angry, we will tend to deny the anger that is in us. (Who, me? I'm not ANGRY!) But we will also tend to feel that everybody around us is angry at us. What we fail to accept in ourselves we tend to project upon others, and in so doing we push them away and keep ourselves from accepting the love they may be giving us. When we are bent upon trying to prove our worth, trying to make ourselves worthy of love, almost everything we do keeps us from accepting the love that's offered to us.

You may remember the story Jesus told of two brothers—often called the parable of the prodigal son—found in Luke 15:11-32. The younger brother left home and made a mess of his life. The older brother stayed home, did everything he was "supposed" to do to prove his worth. In the process of trying to be such a model son, the older brother probably played a major role in driving his younger

brother out of the house. But you remember how the story ends. The younger brother came to himself and returned home empty-handed to plead for mercy. "I don't deserve your love." But his father met him with open arms and tears of joy. You remember the reaction of the older son, how angry he was at his father for loving his "worthless brother." At the end of the story it is obvious to us that the older brother who had tried so hard to be worthy had not allowed himself to accept the love that had been given to him every day. The effort to earn or deserve or merit love cuts us off from love. Love is accepted as a gift, undeserved, unearned, or not accepted at all.

Most of us know ourselves to be like the older brother in Jesus' story—good sons and daughters. Most of us are reluctant to acknowledge that it is our own goodness that so often keeps us from receiving love as a gift. We cut ourselves off by believing that we have measured up and therefore deserve what we receive, or by feeling that we must measure up in order to deserve love. That's why it is so hard for us to hear the words "God loves you" and to believe them. He loves us not just when we meet the standards, not only when we are lovable, but always, regardless. That's hard to hear and to believe. So hard to believe that many of us don't until, like the younger brother in Jesus' story, we come to the end of our rope. We don't hear until all of our efforts have failed. Yet, we don't have to be that stubborn!

We need not wait until we have exhausted ourselves with effort. We can give up—those are the right words, *give up*—telling ourselves that we've got to make our own worth, create our own significance, fashion enough value for ourselves. We can give that up. Right now. Just as we can give up telling ourselves that we've made such a mess of things that God couldn't be foolish enough to love us. We can give that up too; it's far too presumptuous, the feeling that our sins are so bad that God can't forgive them.

Toward the end of the musical "My Fair Lady," Eliza Doolittle shouts in frustration to Henry Higgins, the man of words, "Don't talk of love. Show me! Show me!" And that, thank God, is what God has done in Jesus. He has shown us. Loved us. The three little words "God loves you" are the most potent words we can hear or speak. In the mystery of our hearing and speaking them they may point

71

us toward the One who has shown us by loving us.

The story Jesus told affirms that the father loved both his boys. The older one pushed that love away by believing he had earned it. The younger one almost didn't come home because he knew he didn't deserve it. Both boys were loved—the one who ran away and made a mess of his life and the one who stayed home trying so hard to be good, good enough. Both boys were loved. God loves us. Period. End of report.